HOT DOGS FROM
Almost
HEAVEN

To: David and Marilee

Enjoy!

Nothing beta than WV Hot Dogs!

HOT DOGS FROM Almost HEAVEN

A Hot Dog Lover's Best Friend!

HARRY LYNCH

QUARRIER PRESS
CHARLESTON, WEST VIRGINIA

Quarrier Press
Charleston, WV

Book and cover design: Mark S. Phillips

ISBN: 1-891852-48-5

Library of Congress Catalog Card Number: 2005909561

10 9 8 7 6 5 4 3 2 1

Printed in Canada

Distributed by:
West Virginia Book Co.
1125 Central Ave.
Charleston, WV 25302
www.wvbookco.com

FOREWORD AND FOREWARNED

Few people are more passionate about their hot dogs than West Virginians. Folks, we take 'em seriously. Ask any relocated mountaineer who has ever tried to buy a hot dog outside of his or her state.

Yes, I know, devotees of Chicago-style hot dogs will fuss with me and claim that it "tain't so." Guys and gals from New York will challenge my assumption and dare me to chomp down on a Coney Island Hot Dog before making such a bold statement. Then there are those from the South who will swear that Georgia Red Hots have the most loyal following.

All I can say is . . . Bring 'em on! Let's have a hot dog competition. We'll try yours and you try ours. When we're finished, we'll do it again. The point is . . . There are great tasting hot dogs throughout America, and if you're passionate about your favorite, like I'm passionate about mine, everybody wins!

That's why I've included recipes from all across the USA. Granted, the bulk of the chili sauces come from West Virginia, but I've added some from New York, Ohio, California, even from Australia. And, yes, Chicago, I have your famous "dog" recipe included.

One final word about West Virginia Hot Dogs. We don't worry as much about the wiener as we do the toppings and the bun. We like our buns steamed, our chili smooth, our onions finely chopped and, most of all, we like a final topping of creamy cole slaw down the middle . . . Now, that's worthy of our passion.

v

TABLE OF CONTENTS

ACKNOWLEDGEMENTS, RESOURCES AND JUST PLAIN OLD THANK YOU'S!

There are so many people and organizations to thank whenever you do a compilation of recipes. Even if you don't use a specific recipe from a source, that source may trigger a new recipe or a unique approach. Other times, the recipe might be right on, but lack specific detail on portions or have eccentric directions. I had one recipe given me by an older lady that called for a heaping cupful of chili powder. Another submission said "get the meat good and wet!"

At the risk of overlooking a valuable source—and with due apologies if I do—here's a list of resources that were indispensable in the creation of this book: Lu Rhoades, sister-in-law and librarian who directed me to many sources; Becky Williams; the Prelaz Family; Delmar Robinson; Ellen Stillwell; the Anderson Family, Sharon Royster, and Judy Grigoraci.

Magazines and books and newspapers that were useful include Food TV; *The Charleston Gazette*; *Gourmet* magazine; *Ladies' Home Journal*; *Better Homes and Gardens New Cookbook*; the *Weston Democrat*; *Cookin' From Grandma's Country Kitchen*; and *Campbell's Creative Cooking with Soup*.

Other sources I used were Recipe Source; Food Down Under; Taste of Home; United Methodist Women of Bridgeport; The F.U.N. Place; Millers Hot Dogs; Golden Bowl Recipes; FHA of West Virginia.

Last but certainly not least, I thank my wife and family who endured more than their share of wieners on a bun as this book was constructed.

WHERE THE WIENER MEETS THE BUN

THIS THING CALLED A HOT DOG!

Gosh, folks from all over like to lay claim to "inventing" the hot dog. According to the National Hot Dog and Sausage Council, the city of Frankfurt-am-Main in Germany is traditionally credited with originating the frankfurter. However, the city of Coburg, Germany says, "Not so!" They insist that Johann Georghehner invented the dog in the late 1600s, and that he later traveled to Frankfurt to promote his new product. But hiding in the wings are the good folks from Vienna, Austria, who simply point out that the generic name for the frankfurter, "wiener," is an obvious reference to their fair city.

Here, in North America, hot dog historians debate mightily the origins of the hot dog as we now know it. Who was first to serve it in a bun? Who named it a hot dog? Which ballpark served it first? Did Nathan Handwerker really serve the first hot dog with chili on it at Coney Island?

Don't expect answers to those questions here. I don't know. I'm just thankful that someone, somewhere, came up with the idea of putting a wiener on a soft bun slathered with catsup, mustard, meat sauce, onion, cole slaw, pickle relish, hot peppers, tomato slices . . . and anything else that tweaks the taste buds. My hat's off to them whoever and wherever they are!

The American hot dog—no doubt in my mind—is a culinary culmination of all their efforts and creativity. And, to prove their efforts were on the mark, here are some hot numbers to digest.

The National Hot Dog and Sausage Council estimated

that we eat 20 billion—count 'em—hot dogs a year, and that they are served in 95% of all homes. Two million of those hot dogs are purchased at Chicago's O'Hare airport!

Now, let's talk nutrition.

You'll not find a nutritional analysis at the bottom of each recipe printed in this book. Rather I'm going to do it once, and only once. Yes, there will be slight variations, depending on which ingredients you choose to put on top of your hot dog. Nevertheless, you'll have the basics. So, here goes:

A regular meat hot dog served on a standard bun with catsup, mustard, meat sauce, and chopped onions is approximately 300 calories and contains 17 grams of fat. The wiener will account for 150, more or less, of those calories. Add 100 for the bun.

There you have it! A ton of taste with a smidgen of calories! Obviously, that's my assessment, and probably would come into dispute among some of those in the medical community. So be it. I'll apologize when it's time for my annual physical.

In the meantime, don't get too hung up on the history or the calories of the wiener. Just enjoy!

SAUCES, TOPPINGS AND THOSE AND THOSE LITTLE GREEN THINGS YOU PUT ON TOP

LET'S START AT THE TOP!

If the wiener is the heart of the hot dog, then the topping has to be its soul!

Where I grew up in West Virginia, the topping was more important than the frankfurter. Restaurants were judged by their hot dog chili, not by the meat stick inside. Folks tried to duplicate their favorites, usually without much success. Occasionally, family members would succumb to community pressure and release their family's recipe, knowing full well that once it is released, it belongs to everyone who wants it.

Such was the case with Anderson's, a restaurant that served thousands of hot dogs to the people in and around Weston, West Virginia. Several years after the restaurant had closed, the family members had the recipe printed in the local paper for all to enjoy. I count myself as one of those lucky ones who read it and saved it.

While I'm on the subject of restaurant hot dogs, I need to point out that many of the recipes identified as "restaurant" are probably clones or "taste-a-likes." Although such recipes were shared with me as being authentic, I had no way of verifying that authenticity, since most of the establishments are no longer in business. I did, however, try them all and they were all worthy of inclusion.

I also want to talk about "ownership." Almost all of the recipes in this book were inspired by others. A few are exact reproductions. In those cases where I duplicate a recipe, I do identify the source and give credit to the author, the newspaper or the cookbook. If by some chance, a recipe appears in this book that resembles an old family tradition, call it coincidence. That's the nature of old family favorites. Oftentimes, they have their beginnings in some now obscure publication and are passed generation to generation. The author becomes unknown, and the recipe is crowded into that abyss known as "Public Domain." Then it belongs to everybody.

So much for the technical talk. Let's get back to the sauces.

Which topping is my favorite? I'm going to cop out on this one. I really don't know. It depends on the mood I'm in. Sometimes, I tend toward the spicy. Other times, I'm looking for mild. I may opt for a Chicago style dog, or try one of the onion sauces. All of the recipes are someone's favorite. That's why they are included.

I do know I remember well the hot dogs I devoured as a kid. I think I have been searching for that "taste" ever since. I also remember I paid as little as ten cents for a hot dog with chili and onions. I keep searching for that price as well! Odds are I will never match the price, but I have come close to matching the flavors of my past. I hope you, also, will find a recipe in this chapter that will bring back a memory or two. And, if you find a hot dog for a dime . . . keep it to yourself and enjoy!

HILLBILLY HOT DOG CHILI

1 lb. ground beef
2 cups water
1 1/2 tsp. chili powder
1 tsp. salt
1/2 tsp. black pepper
1/2 cup catsup
1/4 cup honey

Place ground beef in a 3 quart saucepan. Cover with water. Bring to a boil, then reduce heat to low. Simmer covered for 1 hour. Add the remaining ingredients. Simmer for another 45 – 60 minutes, or until desired consistency is reached. Add more water if needed. Makes 18 – 20 servings.

BASIC HOT DOG SAUCE

1 lb. ground beef
2 cups water
1 can (12 oz.) tomato paste
1 small onion, chopped
1 tbs. chili powder
1 tsp. pepper
2 tsp. salt

Place ground beef and water in a 2 quart saucepan. Work with hands until blended. Place over medium high heat to bring to a boil. Reduce heat and simmer for 30 minutes. Add tomato paste, chopped onion, salt, pepper and chili powder. Simmer for another 30 minutes or until right consistency is reached. Makes 18 – 20 servings.

BEEF AND BEAN HOT DOG CHILI

2 lbs. ground beef
1 medium onion, chopped finely
1 clove garlic, minced
3 cups water
1 15.5 oz. can tomato sauce
2 tbs. chili powder
1 tbs. vinegar
1 tbs. Worcestershire sauce
1 tbs. black pepper
1 16 oz. can pinto beans, drained

In a 4 quart stockpot, brown the ground beef with the onion and garlic until meat is no longer pink in the center. Drain. Return meat to stockpot, add the remaining ingredients, bring to a boil, reduce heat and simmer for at least 1 hour, or until desired consistency is reached. Makes 20 servings.

BUBBA'S ZESTY HOT DOG SAUCE

1 1/2 lbs. ground beef
3 cups water
1/4 cup finely chopped yellow onion
2 tbs. chili powder
1 tsp. ground black pepper
1 tbs. red pepper flakes
1 tsp. salt
1 15.5 oz. can tomato sauce
1/4 cup finely ground cracker crumbs

Put ground beef in a two quart saucepan. Add the water and chopped onion. Stir to blend well. Cover. Bring mixture to a boil over medium high heat, then reduce to medium low. Simmer for 45 minutes, stirring occasionally. Add chili powder, black pepper, red pepper flakes, salt and tomato sauce. Continue simmering, uncovered, for 1 to 1 1/2 hours. Add cracker crumbs, stir to mix well. Remove from heat. Makes 20 – 25 servings.

BETTER HOMES & GARDENS CONEY ISLAND SAUCE

1/2 lb. ground beef
1/4 cup water
1/4 cup chopped onion
1 clove garlic, minced
1 8 oz. can tomato sauce
1/2 tsp. chili powder
1/2 tsp. monosodium glutamate
1/2 tsp. salt

In a medium skillet, brown the ground beef thoroughly, breaking up meat with a fork until fine. Add remaining ingredients. Simmer uncovered for 10 minutes. Makes 10 servings.

CINCINNATI STYLE HOT DOG SAUCE

1 lb. ground chuck
1 large onion, finely diced
2 cloves garlic, minced
1/2 cup catsup
1/2 cup water
1 cup purchased sweet BBQ sauce
1 tsp. black pepper
1/2 tsp. cumin
1/2 tsp. cinnamon
1/4 tsp. ground cloves
1 tbs. chili powder
2 tbs. grated unsweetened chocolate
1/2 tsp. salt

Brown ground chuck—stirring often to break up meat —over medium high heat in a large skillet. Drain well. Add the catsup, water and barbecue sauce. Stir to blend. Add the remaining ingredients. Bring to a boil, reduce heat and simmer for 15 minutes, or until chocolate has melted and the onions are tender. Makes 18 – 20 servings.

CONEY ISLAND
HOT DOG SAUCE

1 lb. ground beef
2 cups water
1 small onion, finely diced
3 tsp. paprika
2 tsp. chili powder
2 tsp. ground cumin
1 tsp. salt
1/2 tsp. cayenne pepper
1/4 tsp. black pepper

Place ground beef and water in a three quart sauce-pan. Blend with hands. Add remaining ingredients, stir and bring to a slight boil over medium heat. Reduce to simmer and cook for 1 hour, stirring frequently. Makes 10 – 12 servings.

CONEY ISLAND
HOT DOG SAUCE #2

1/4 cup ground beef
1 1/2 cups water
1 6 oz. can tomato paste
1/4 cup sweet pickle relish
1 tbs. chopped onion
1 tbs. prepared mustard
1 tbs. Worcestershire sauce
2 tsp. chili powder
1 tsp. salt
2 tsp. sugar

Place ground beef in a medium size skillet over medium high heat. Fry until meat is no longer pink. While meat is cooking, stir to break up. Drain. Add water and the remaining ingredients. Bring to a boil, reduce heat and simmer uncovered for 30 – 45 minutes. Makes 10 – 12 servings.

CROCK POT HOT DOG CHILI

3 lbs. ground chuck
2 cloves garlic, minced
1 tbs. chili powder
1 tbs. ground cumin
1 tsp. dried oregano
2 cups water
2 cans (10.5 oz. each) condensed beef
broth

In a large skillet, brown the ground chuck until no longer pink. Drain. Transfer meat to a crock pot (slow cooker). Add the remaining ingredients. Stir. Cook on low for 6-8 hours. Makes about 30 – 35 servings.

CROCK POT HOT DOG CHILI #2

3 lbs. ground chuck
3 cups water
3 cloves garlic, minced
2 tsp. salt
2 tbs. chili powder
1/4 cup paprika
1/4 tsp. cayenne pepper

In a large skillet, brown ground chuck over medium high heat until no longer pink. Place in a medium sized crock pot (slow cooker) with the remaining ingredients. Stir to blend well. Cover and cook on low heat for 8 – 10 hours.

CROCK POT HOT DOG CHILI #3

3 lbs ground beef
1 onion, chopped
2 cups water
1 28 oz. bottle catsup
1/4 cup prepared mustard
1 package taco seasoning mix
1/2 cup brown sugar
1/2 tsp. salt
1/4 tsp. pepper

In a large skillet, brown ground beef with the onion over medium heat. Stir in remaining ingredients. Place in a crock pot. Cook over low heat for 6 – 7 hours. Makes approximately 35 servings.

DELMER ROBINSON'S HOT DOG CHILI

1 lb. ground chuck
1 medium onion, chopped
1 small can tomato paste
3 cans water (use tomato paste can)
1/2 cup catsup
1 tsp. vinegar
1 tsp. salt
1 1/2 tbs. chili powder.

Combine all of the ingredients in a 3 quart saucepan. Add the water one can at a time. Stir after each addition. Cook slowly over low heat for 1 to 1 1/2 hours. Makes 18 – 20 servings.

DETROIT CITY HOT DOG SAUCE

1 lb. ground beef
2 cups water
5 tbs. chili powder
3 tbs. paprika
1 tbs. dry mustard
1/2 tsp. salt
1/4 tsp. black pepper

Place ground beef in a large skillet. Add the water and the remaining spices and seasonings. Stir well. Simmer over medium low heat for approximately one hour or until right consistency is reached. Makes 10 – 12 servings.

GARDEN VARIETY
HOT DOG TOPPING

2 1/2 tbs. yellow mustard
1 cup sweet pickle relish
1 small onion, finely chopped
1 small green bell pepper, finely
    chopped
2 Roma tomatoes, seeded and finely
    chopped

Arrange the toppings in the above order. After wiener is placed in the bun, apply the toppings one at a time. Makes approximately 8 servings.

FREEZER HOT DOG CHILI

1/4 lb. lard
1 medium onion, chopped
3 cloves garlic, minced
6 tbs. hot chili powder
2 cups water
5 lbs. ground chuck
1/4 tsp. allspice
1/2 cup cracker meal
1 tbs. paprika
2 tsp. salt
1 tsp. black pepper

In a heavy 5 quart Dutch oven, melt the lard over medium heat. Add the chopped onion and garlic cloves. Saute for five minutes. Add water and ground chuck. Mix well. Cook for 10 minutes, stirring constantly. Cover pan and simmer for 30 minutes. Add remaining ingredients. Stir. Remove from heat. Pour into a 9 x 13 inch shallow pan to cool. Let set until it can be cut into 2 inch squares. Wrap in foil. Store in freezer. Thaw in microwave or on stove to use. One square makes enough for 4 hot dogs.

GOURMET MAGAZINE'S HOT DOG SAUCE

2 garlic cloves, minced
1/2 cup finely chopped onion
2 tbs. vegetable oil
1 lb. lean ground beef
1 tsp. salt
1/2 tsp. black pepper
1 tbs. yellow mustard
1 tbs. vinegar
1 tsp. Worcestershire sauce
1/2 tsp. Tabasco, or to taste
1/4 cup catsup
1/2 to 1 cup tomato juice

In large skillet, cook garlic and onion in oil over moderate heat, until onion is softened. Add beef and cook, stirring and breaking up any lumps with a fork. Add remaining ingredients, adding enough juice to create a spoonable mixture. Simmer for 10 minutes. Makes enough sauce for 6 servings.

HAWAIIAN HOT DOG SAUCE

1 cup apricot preserves
1/2 cup tomato sauce
1/3 cup vinegar
2 tbs. soy sauce
2 tbs. honey
1 tbs. light olive oil
1 tsp. salt
1/4 tsp. ground ginger
1/4 cup pineapple juice

In a small saucepan, combine all of the ingredients. Place over medium low heat. Simmer for 10 minutes, stirring often. Makes 8 – 10 servings.

TOLEDO STYLE HOT DOG CHILI

2 lbs. ground chuck
2 cups water
3 tbs. chili powder
1 tbs. paprika
1 tbs. black pepper
1 tsp. onion powder
1 tsp. garlic powder
1/2 tbs. thyme
1/2 tbs. cumin
1 tsp. brown sugar
1/4 tsp. cayenne pepper

Brown meat in a large skillet or stockpot over medium high heat. Drain. Add remaining ingredients. Stir well. Simmer for 1 hour. Makes 20 servings.

QUICK HOT DOG CHILI

1 lb. ground chuck
2 cups water
1 can condensed tomato soup
1 small onion, chopped
2 tbs. chili powder

Place ground chuck in a 2 quart saucepan. Cover the meat with the water. Bring to a boil over medium high heat. Reduce heat and simmer for 30 minutes. Add chopped onion, chili powder and tomato soup. Cook for another 20 minutes, stirring often. Makes about 18 – 20 servings.

QUICK HOT DOG CHILI #2

1 lb. ground chuck
1 medium onion, finely diced
1 tbs. chili powder
1/2 tsp. paprika
1/8 tsp. garlic powder
1 small can (6 oz.) tomato paste
2 cups water

In a medium skillet, brown ground chuck and diced onions. Add chili powder, paprika, garlic powder, tomato paste and water. Cover and simmer for 2 hours, stirring often. Add more water if sauce becomes too thick. Makes 12 – 15 servings.

HOT DOG ONION SAUCE

2 tbs. vegetable oil
2 medium yellow onions, cut into
   1/4 inch slices
1/4 cup catsup
1/8 tsp. ground cinnamon
1/8 tsp. chili powder
Dash of hot pepper sauce
1/4 tsp. salt
1/2 cup water

In medium sized skillet, heat the vegetable oil over medium heat. Add the onion and fry for 6 – 7 minutes until golden and limp. Mix in the catsup. Add the cinnamon, chili powder, pepper sauce and salt. Pour in the water. Bring to a boil, reduce heat and simmer, uncovered, for 10 minutes. Makes 6 – 8 servings.

KANSAS CITY HOT DOG CHILI

2 lbs. ground beef
8 oz. tomato sauce
8 oz. tomato paste
2 cups water
2 tsp. chili powder
1/2 tsp. salt
1/4 tsp. pepper
1 tbs. hot sauce
1/2 cup sweet barbecue sauce

Mix all of the ingredients in a 5 quart stockpot. Stir well before placing on heat. Bring to a slight boil, reduce heat to low, and simmer uncovered for 1 hour or until desired consistency is reached. Makes 20 – 25 servings.

LADIES' HOME JOURNAL HOT DOG CHILI

1/2 lb. ground beef
1 small onion, chopped
1 small green bell pepper, chopped
1 clove garlic, crushed
1 tbs. chili powder
1 can (16 oz.) crushed tomatoes
1 tbs. tomato paste
1 tsp. salt
1/8 tsp. ground red pepper

In a large skillet, brown the ground beef over medium high heat. Add onion, peppers, garlic and chili powder. Cook for 3 – 4 minutes longer. Stir in tomatoes and their juice, tomato paste, ground red pepper and salt. Bring to boil, reduce heat and simmer uncovered for 10 minutes. Makes 4 – 6 servings.

LOWER FAT HOT DOG CHILI

1 lb. extra lean ground beef (7% fat)
1 tbs. olive oil
1 large onion, chopped
1 green bell pepper, chopped
1 medium carrot, finely shredded
1 stalk celery, chopped
2 cloves garlic, minced
1 tbs. chili powder
1 tbs. sweet pickle relish
2 tbs. prepared mustard
1 1/2 cups catsup
1/4 cup water

In a large non-stick skillet, brown the extra lean ground beef in the olive oil. Drain well. Add the chopped onion, bell pepper, carrot, celery and garlic. Continue cooking for another 5 minutes. Stir in the chili powder, mustard, pickle relish, water and catsup. Simmer for ten minutes. Makes 10 – 12 servings.

LU'S HOT DOG SAUCE

1 1/2 lbs. ground chuck
3 cups water
1 can (10 oz.) condensed tomato soup
3/4 cup catsup
2 tbs. chili powder
1 tsp. sugar
1/2 tsp. salt
1/4 tsp. pepper

Place ground chuck in a 4 quart saucepan. Cover with the water. Mix with hands. Bring to a boil over medium high heat, reduce to medium low and cook for 45 minutes or until meat is fine and light brown in color. Add remaining ingredients, cover, and cook for approximately 2 more hours or until right consistency is reached. Makes 18 – 20 servings.

MANHATTAN HOT DOG CHILI

1/2 lb. ground round
3 cups water
12 oz. (2 small cans) tomato paste
1/2 cup sweet pickle relish
2 tbs. chopped onion
2 tbs. prepared mustard
2 tbs. Worcestershire sauce
2 tbs. chili powder
2 tsp. sugar
1 tsp. salt

Place meat in a 4 quart pan. Brown over medium high heat until no longer pink. Add water, bring to a boil, then lower heat to a simmer. Cook uncovered for 30 minutes. Add remaining ingredients and cook uncovered for another 30 minutes. Makes about 10 servings.

MILLER'S HOT DOG BARBECUE SAUCE

3/4 cup chopped onion
3 tbs. butter or margarine
1 1/2 cups chopped celery
1 1/2 cups catsup
3/4 cup water
1/3 cup lemon juice
3 tbs. brown sugar
3 tbs. vinegar
1 tbs. Worcestershire sauce
1 tbs. yellow mustard

In a large saucepan, sauté the onion in the butter until tender. Add celery, catsup, water, lemon juice, brown sugar, vinegar, Worcestershire sauce and mustard. Bring to a boil, cover, reduce heat and simmer for 30 minutes. Makes 16 servings.

NEW YORK, NEW YORK HOT DOG SAUCE

1 package onion soup mix
1 cup very hot water
1/2 lb. ground beef
1 tbs. vegetable shortening
1 tsp. chili powder
1 cup catsup
1/2 tsp. salt

In a medium bowl, add the soup mix to the hot water. Let sit for 15 minutes. Strain onion pieces from soup. In a medium skillet, add the shortening and melt over medium heat. Put in the ground beef and brown until no longer pink. Add chili powder, catsup, salt and reserved liquid from soup mix. Simmer for about 30 minutes. Makes 10 servings.

NEW YORKER HOT DOG CHILI

1 lb. ground chuck
1 small onion, chopped
1 clove garlic, minced
1/2 cup beef broth
1 tbs. natural soy sauce
2 tsp. chili powder
1 tsp. allspice
1 tsp. cumin
1/2 tsp. each of black pepper, nutmeg
    and celery salt

In a large skillet, brown the ground chuck. Add the chopped onion and minced garlic during the last 5 minutes of browning. Drain excess fat. Add the remaining ingredients, stirring well. Simmer for 10 – 15 minutes, or until liquid is almost evaporated. Transfer mixture to a food processor and pulse 5 – 6 times, or until meat is finely ground. Makes 10 servings.

NYC PUSHCART
HOT DOG RELISH

1/2 cup water
1 medium onion, chopped
1/3 cup catsup
1/4 cup cider vinegar
1 tsp. Coleman's dry mustard
1 tsp. paprika

Place all ingredients in a medium saucepan. Bring to a boil over medium high heat. Reduce to simmer and cook for 15 – 20 minutes or until desired consistency is reached. Makes 6 – 8 servings.

ONION HOT DOG CHILI

1/2 lb. ground beef
1 large sweet onion, sliced thin
1/2 small green bell pepper, sliced thin
1/2 cup catsup
2 tsp. chili powder
1/2 tsp. salt
1/4 tsp. cayenne pepper

In a medium skillet, brown ground beef until no longer pink. Drain excess grease. Add the thinly sliced onion and pepper and continue cooking until onion is transparent. Add catsup, chili powder, salt and cayenne pepper. Simmer for 5 more minutes. Makes 8 – 10 servings.

PICANTE AND BEEF HOT DOG SAUCE

1/2 lb. ground chuck
2 tbs. minced onion
1 cup medium picante sauce

Brown ground chuck with onions over medium heat. Drain. Return meat to skillet and add the picante sauce. Simmer over medium low heat for 8 – 10 minutes or until desired consistency is reached. Makes 8 – 10 servings.

PIZZA DOG SAUCE

1 15.5 oz. can tomato sauce
1 tsp. Italian blend seasoning
1/4 tsp. garlic powder
1/4 tsp. salt
1/8 tsp. onion powder
1/8 tsp. black pepper
1 tbs. light olive oil

Put tomato sauce and dry ingredients in a small saucepan. Bring to a slight boil, reduce heat and simmer for 15 minutes. Stir in 1 tablespoon of light olive oil.

POOL HALL HOT DOG CHILI

2 lbs. ground beef
4 cups water
5 small onions, diced
1/2 cup prepared mustard
2 tbs. sugar
1 tbs. cider vinegar
2 cups catsup
4 tsp. chili powder
2 tsp. salt

Put ground beef and water in a 4 quart stockpot. Mix with hands to a smooth consistency. Add the remaining ingredients. Bring to a boil, reduce heat and simmer for 1 – 1 1/2 hours. Add more water if necessary. Makes 25 – 30 servings.

PORK HOT DOG CHILI

1 lb. lean ground pork
1/4 cup dried, minced onion flakes
2 cups water
2 tbs. chili powder
1/2 tsp. garlic powder
1 cup catsup
1/2 tsp. salt
1/2 tsp. crushed red pepper flakes

Place pork, onion flakes and water in a four quart saucepan. Bring to a boil, reduce heat and simmer for 1 hour. Add the remaining ingredients. Return to a simmer and cook for an additional 1 hour or until right consistency is reached. Makes 16 – 20 servings.

SAUERKRAUT HOT DOG TOPPING

15 oz. sauerkraut, drained and rinsed
1/4 cup sweet pickle relish
2 tbs. brown sugar
1 tbs. prepared mustard
1/2 tsp. caraway seed

Place all ingredients in a medium saucepan. Stir to combine. Cook over low heat until heated through. Makes 8 – 10 servings.

TASTE OF HOME HOT DOG CHILI

1 lb. ground beef
1 clove garlic, minced
1 cup tomato juice
1 can (6 oz.) tomato paste
2 tbs. chili powder
1 tsp. hot sauce
1 tsp. salt
1/4 tsp. pepper

In large skillet, brown ground beef with garlic. Drain. Stir in next six ingredients. Simmer, uncovered, for 20 minutes. Makes 10 – 12 servings.

TAXI STAND HOT DOG SAUCE

1 lb. ground beef
2 cups water
1/4 cup finely chopped onion
14 oz. catsup
2 tbs. chili powder
1 tsp. salt
1/2 tsp. ground black pepper
1/4 cup cracker crumbs

Place ground beef in a two quart saucepan. Add water. Bring to a boil, reduce heat and simmer uncovered for 45 minutes. Add chopped onion, catsup, chili powder, salt and black pepper. Continue cooking, stirring often for 1 hour. Add cracker crumbs, stir and remove from heat. Makes 20 servings.

TURN UP THE HEAT
HOT DOG SAUCE

1 lb. ground beef
2 1/2 cups water
2 tbs. dried, minced onions
8 oz. can tomato sauce
4 oz. catsup (1/2 of tomato sauce can)
2 tbs. chili powder
1 tbs. crushed red pepper
1 tsp. black pepper
1 tsp. salt
1/4 cup cracker crumbs*

Place ground beef in a two quart saucepan. Cover with the water. Add the minced onions. Bring to a boil, reduce heat and cook for 45 minutes. Add next six ingredients. Hold the cracker crumbs. Cover pan and simmer for another hour. Add cracker crumbs, stir well to mix. Remove from heat. Add more water if too thick. Makes 20 servings.

*Put 5 saltines in food processor and grind until fine.

UPSTATE NEW YORK
HOT DOG SAUCE

1 lb. ground beef
1 tsp. salt
1 tsp. black pepper
2 tbs. chili powder
1 tsp. crushed red pepper
1 tsp. paprika
1/4 tsp. cinnamon
1 small can (8 oz.) tomato sauce
1 quart water

Brown ground beef in a large skillet over medium high heat. Add the dry ingredients. Stir to blend well. Pour in the water, then add the tomato sauce. Bring to a boil, reduce heat and simmer for 2 – 3 hours, or until desired consistency is reached. Makes 18 – 20 servings.

VEGETARIAN HOT DOG SAUCE

2 tbs. canola oil
1 medium tomato, chopped
1/4 cup chopped onion
1/4 cup chopped green bell pepper
1 clove garlic, minced
1 can (10 3/4 oz.) condensed tomato
   soup
1/4 tsp. hot pepper sauce
1 tbs. vinegar
1/2 tsp. dried thyme

In a two quart saucepan, sautée in oil the tomato, onion, green bell pepper and garlic over medium heat until vegetables are tender. Stir in the soup, hot pepper sauce, vinegar and thyme. Heat to boiling. Reduce heat to low and simmer, uncovered, for 10 – 15 minutes, stirring occasionally. Makes about 16 servings.

ZESTY VIKING HOT DOG SAUCE

3 lbs. ground round
2 medium onions, chopped
2 cups water
3 tbs. prepared mustard
3 tbs. vinegar
2 cups tomato sauce
3 tbs. chili powder
3 cloves minced garlic
1 tbs. crushed red pepper
1/2 tsp. cayenne pepper
1 tsp. salt

Place ground round, onions and water in a 5 quart stockpot. Bring to a boil over medium high heat, then lower heat to a simmer. Cover and cook for 30 minutes. Add remaining ingredients and cook slowly for one hour, stirring often.

HOMEMADE HOT DOG RELISH

1 lb. sweet onions
1 lb. green bell peppers
1 lb. red bell peppers
1 cup cider vinegar
3 tbs. sugar
1/4 tsp. mustard seed
1/4 tsp. celery seed
1/4 tsp. dry mustard
2 tsp. salt

Finely chop the onions, green and red bell peppers. Place in large mixing bowl. In a small saucepan, combine the next 6 ingredients. Bring to a slight boil, stirring constantly. Remove from heat and pour over chopped vegetables, stirring to blend. Cover and place in refrigerator until completely cooled. Makes 18 – 20 servings.

HOT DOG CHILI FOR A CROWD #1

If you've ever been asked to make hot dog chili for a crowd, you know the agonizing moment you experience as you try to convert the family recipe from 10 servings to 100. Well, fear no more. Here are some pre-measured examples for you to enjoy.

20 lbs. ground beef
3 quarts water
3 cans (15.5 oz.) tomato sauce
1 cup chili powder
1/4 cup salt
2 tbs. black pepper
1 tbs. sugar

Place ground beef in a 16 quart stockpot. Add water. Mix by hand until blended with the meat. Bring to a slight boil over medium high heat. Cover pan, reduce heat and simmer for 30 minutes. Add tomato sauce, chili powder, salt, pepper and sugar. Stir, and continue simmering—covered—for 2 – 3 hours. Makes sauce for 350 hot dogs.

HOT DOG CHILI FOR A CROWD #2

10 lbs. ground beef
3 medium onions, chopped
2 gallons tomato sauce
4 tsp. chili powder
4 tsp. dried oregano
2 tsp. salt
1/2 cup sugar
6 tbs. black pepper

In a 16 quart stockpot, brown the ground beef with the chopped onions over medium high heat until meat is no longer pink. Add the tomato sauce and the remaining dry ingredients. Simmer 3 – 5 hours or until desired consistency is reached. Makes 200 – 225 servings.

HOT DOG CHILI FOR A CROWD #3

10 lbs. ground beef
2 quarts water
10 tbs. sugar
5 tbs. chili powder
5 tbs. salt
30 oz. (5 small cans) tomato paste

Place all of the ingredients in a 16 quart stockpot. Mix well. Place over low heat and cook for 2 hours or more, or until right consistency is reached. Press with a potato masher frequently to break up meat. Add more water if necessary. Makes approximately 200 servings.

STATE FAIR HOT DOG CHILI FOR A CROWD

5 lbs. ground beef
4 cups water
3 medium onions, chopped
2 cups tomato paste
8 cups catsup
4 tbs. chili powder
1 tbs. salt
1 tsp. black pepper

Combine ground beef, water and onions in a large stockpot. Mix well. Cook over medium low heat until beef is brown (about 45 minutes). Add remaining ingredients. Again, mix well. Simmer uncovered for about 1 hour or until desired consistency is reached. Makes approximately 75 servings.

UNCLE HARRY'S AND DADDY'S HOT DOG CHILI FOR A CROWD

5 lbs. ground beef
2 quarts water
3 medium onions, finely minced
1/4 cup brown sugar
1/4 cup cider vinegar
2 tbs. prepared mustard
2 tbs. chili powder
1 1/2 tsp. garlic powder
1 tsp. ground celery seed
5 large cans (15.5 oz.) tomato sauce
2 tsp. salt
1 tsp. black pepper
1 tsp. crushed red pepper flakes

In a large stockpot combine the ground beef and water. Bring to a boil over medium high heat, reduce heat to low and simmer for 1 hour. Add the remainder of the ingredients. Continue to cook, stirring often, for 1 – 2 hours, or until desired consistency. Serves 100.

SOME OF MY FAVORITES
FROM RESTAURANTS

The next few pages contain recipes that came from restaurants. Many of these establishments no longer exist, but the memories of, and recipes for, their hot dogs have survived.

WEST VIRGINIA RESTAURANT STYLE HOT DOG SAUCE

5 lbs. ground beef
2 quarts water
3 tbs. chili powder
2 tbs. sugar
2 tbs. salt
2 tbs. black pepper
1 tbs. crushed red pepper
1 15.5 oz. can tomato sauce
15 oz. catsup

Place ground beef and water in large stockpot. Blend mixture with hands. Place over medium high heat. Bring to a boil, reduce heat to medium and boil for 1 hour. Add the remaining ingredients, stir, reduce heat to low and simmer for another hour or until desired consistency is reached. Add water if necessary. Makes 80 servings.

ANDERSON'S RESTAURANT HOT DOG CHILI

3 lbs. ground beef
3 cups water
2 tbs. chili powder
1 tbs. salt
1 tsp. hot pepper sauce
2 tbs. minced onion
1 tsp. minced garlic
1 can (7 oz.) Contadina tomato paste
1/2 can vinegar

Place all of the ingredients in a large stockpot. Mix well. Place over medium high heat. Bring to a slight boil, reduce heat to simmer and cook for 3 – 4 hours, or until desired consistency is reached. Add more water if necessary. Makes approximately 50 servings.

RESTAURANT HOT DOG CHILI #1

4 lbs. ground beef
1 1/2 quarts water
15 oz. catsup
1 can (15.5 oz.) tomato sauce
3 tbs. chili powder
2 tbs. black pepper
2 tbs. sugar

Place ground beef and water in a 5 quart stockpot. Blend with hands. Bring to a boil over medium high heat. Cover, reduce heat and simmer for 45 minutes. Add the catsup, tomato sauce, chili powder, black pepper and sugar. Continue cooking for 2 hours or until sauce is the right consistency. Makes enough sauce for 75 – 80 hot dogs.

RESTAURANT HOT DOG CHILI #2

10 lbs. ground beef
2 quarts water
1 gallon tomato puree
8 tbs. chili powder
8 tbs. salt
8 tbs. black pepper
1 gallon onions, finely chopped

Place ground beef in 16 quart stock pot. Add the water. Blend with hands. Bring to a boil over medium heat, then reduce to a simmer. Cook at low temperature for 1 hour covered. Add tomato puree, chili powder, salt, black pepper and onions. Cook uncovered over low heat for 1 – 2 hours, or until right consistency is reached. Makes 180 – 200 servings.

RESTAURANT HOT DOG CHILI #3

3 lbs. ground beef, browned and drained
1 stick margarine
1 tbs. garlic powder
1 quart tomato juice
3 tbs. chili powder
1 tbs. salt
1 tbs. sugar
1 tsp. cayenne pepper
1/2 tsp. black pepper

Brown ground beef in a 5 quart stockpot. Drain well. Add the remainder of the ingredients. Bring to a boil, reduce heat and simmer for 1 1/2 hours. Makes 25 – 30 servings.

RESTAURANT HOT DOG CHILI #4 CIRCA 1939

1 lb. ground beef
6 small onions, minced
4 cloves garlic, minced
1 tsp. chili powder
1 tsp. paprika
4 tbs. vinegar
1 tbs. prepared mustard
2 tbs. brown sugar
1 tbs. celery seed
1 quart canned tomatoes

In a large skillet, brown meat, crumbling into small pieces. Add the remaining ingredients, bring to a boil, then simmer for 1 hour or until chili is thickened. Cut tomatoes with edge of soup spoon while chili is cooking. Makes 12 – 15 servings.

THE WIENER, THE BUN, THE FUN OF PUTTING IT ALL TOGETHER!

A BAKER'S DOZEN OF HOT DOG RECIPES FROM ACROSS AMERICA

Sauces, toppings, steamed buns and wieners are nothing more than grocery cart items until somebody slaps them together in an orderly fashion and calls them Hot Dogs!

I've put together 13 examples (including one that shies away from the bun) of wiener "slapping" techniques that will pique your curiosity, if not your taste buds. It's not likely you'll find all of these assemblages to your liking, but, hopefully, you'll find one or two recipes on the following pages that you'll "dog ear" for future reference.

WEST VIRGINIA DOG

While folks in Chicago might truly like their hot dogs, the people in West Virginia downright praise their versions of this all American sandwich. Virtually every small town in West Virginia boasts of a restaurant that makes the "best hot dog" around. And, chances are, they're all right.

What separates the West Virginia Dog from its meaty cousins up North is the addition of a creamy cole slaw to the toppings. It's not a requirement, but ask for a hot dog with everything, and the slaw will be there . . . right on top of the mustard, catsup, chili sauce and onions! It's like getting your protein, veggies and roughage all in one delectable bite! Here's how to assemble a hot dog West Virginia style.

Steam a standard bun, or toast an English bun. Boil or fry wiener of your choice. Place in bun. Add mustard and catsup. Spoon on favorite meat sauce. Add chopped onions and spoon on the creamy cole slaw.

COLE SLAW RECIPE:

1/2 head of cabbage, finely shredded. Place in a 2 quart bowl. In another bowl, blend together one half cup mayonnaise (or Miracle Whip), 1 tbs. vinegar, 2 tbs. granulated sugar and 2 tbs. milk. Whip with a fork or wire whisk. Blend with the shredded cabbage.

CHICAGO DOG

The Chicago Dog may be the most unique hot dog in America. Some have described it as a "salad" on a bun. And, to the uninitiated, it might look a little strange. But to those who have savored its uniqueness, it's a culinary delight and well worth the effort to produce.

Chicago claims to have over 4,000 hot dog stands. And, that's not blowing wind from the Windy City. Competition is keen and locals debate vigorously which stand makes the best hot dog. Regardless of who's the best, there are two things common to Chicago Hot Dogs: a steamed poppyseed bun and an all beef (probably Vienna brand) wiener. Here's two versions: First, the traditional style; Second, a variation for those of us who can't get to Chicago.

Traditional Version: **Steamed poppyseed bun. Grilled, boiled or microwaved Vienna all beef wiener. Cook to 170 degrees internally. Place wiener in bun. Add the following toppings: A generous ribbon of yellow mustard; bright green pickle relish; fresh chopped onions; two tomato wedges; a Kosher pickle spear; two sport peppers (hot, similar to hot salad peppers); and, a sprinkling of celery salt. Now, hold onto it with both hands and enjoy.**

Variation: Use any good hot dog bun, seeded if preferred but not necessary. An all beef wiener is a requirement. Again, buy a good quality wiener here. Add the mustard, green relish, chopped onion, tomato slices, kosher pickle spear, hot pepper rings and, a dash of celery salt (again, a necessity to get the full flavor of a Chicago-style hot dog). Some optional toppings are chopped cucumber, kraut or dill pickle chips that can be substituted for the pickle spear. Not quite authentic, but close enough to experience what folks in Chicago call hot dogs!

BALL PARK HOT DOGS

"Get 'em while they're hot!". . . Just one of the many sounds we associate with America's favorite pastime. Every child and those adults who remember what it was like to be a child can recall the pleasure of eating a ball park hot dog!

The toppings may have been simple, but the taste was explosive, partly because of the quality of wiener that went into the product. Vendors paid good prices for the privilege of selling their dogs at the parks. Consequently, they had to convince the fans the dog was worth the price of admission, so to speak. Here, in all of its simple glory is how to assemble a Ball Park Hot Dog.

Start with a plump, all beef wiener that's filled with flavor. Grill it, lay it in the bun, then spread a generous dollop of yellow mustard down the center of the dog. Add some sweet pickle relish, maybe even some chopped onions. It's worth going to bat for!

CONEY ISLAND DOG

Blame it on Charles Feltman. He's the one who started selling frankfurters at his restaurant on Coney Island in 1871. Then in 1916, Nathan Handwerker decided to sell hot dogs from a small stand near that same location. Between the two, the Coney Island Hot Dog was born. Handwerker, by the way, named his stand Nathan's, which still operates successfully throughout the Northeast. Indeed, Nathan's has expanded and sell their all-beef wieners at many national grocery store chains.

Today, it's hard to define what is a true Coney Island Hot Dog. The most typical characteristic appears to be the meat sauce spread over the top of the wiener. Those sauces, however, may vary. Suffice it to say, pick your favorite from the choices on pages 14 – 15.

Take your choice of wiener. Boil or grill. Place in hot dog bun, spread with mustard, a little catsup and top with favorite meat sauce. Meat sauce may or may not contain beans. Add chopped onions.

HAWAIIAN DOG

O.K., I'll fess up. I don't know if this hot dog is Hawaiian or Californian. I do know that it's an off-the-wall version of a wiener in a bun that'll please some palates. Maybe yours is one of them.

This recipe has more to do with the sauce—or should I say the treatment of the sauce—than with the wiener or the bun. It's a perfect example of thinking outside the box, and or, er, the bun. Like they used to say on TV, "Try it, you'll like it!"

Cut slits on the sides of the wieners. Place on grill and baste with the Hawaiian Hot Dog Sauce found on page 24. When wieners have browned nicely, place in a toasted English bun. Add chopped green bell peppers, diced pineapple and chopped onions. Spread a little more sauce on top. Now, pretend you're relaxing in Honolulu.

LOW CARB DOG

I swore I wouldn't put a dog recipe in this book that wasn't fitted with a bun. I lied. This recipe has been around a long time, well before the low-carb fad showed up on the talk shows. It was a favorite of my kids when they were growing up (Mainly, because it was cheap and easy to make, and fit the budget). My sister calls this recipe Coney Island Quail. That's a bit fancy for my tastes, but if it attracts the more sophisticated readers whose palates are more discriminating than mine, then quail it is.

Choose a wiener of your choice. Split down the center, but do not cut all the way through. Put a narrow stream of catsup down the cut, place thin strips of processed cheddar cheese in the slit. Wrap wiener—spiral fashion—with thinly sliced, hickory smoked bacon. Secure bacon with toothpicks. Place on grill or in skillet and cook until edges turn brown (Some like it slightly blackened). Serve on plate with cheap macaroni (*oops*) and cheese.

MEXI-DOG

Let's go South of the Border for this one . . . A Mexi-Dog. No, it's not a wiener in a taco shell, or a spiced up dog wrapped in a tortilla. It's a legitimate hot dog that's got a southwestern influence.

Hot dog chilies aren't generally as spicy as Texas-style chilies, at least when it comes to chili powder, cumin and hot sauces. However, a grilled and browned wiener wears this topping with all the grace and elegance of a matador standing in the middle of the ring accepting applause from his fans. We think you'll cheer over this version, too.

Choose a wiener of your choice. Grill or pan fry it to get some dark edges. Place in toasted English bun, add a thin stream of catsup. Top with the Picante and Beef Hot Dog Sauce found on page 39. Add chopped onions. Olé!

MILLER'S BARBECUED HOT DOG

O.K., you West Coast fans, here's one for you. Miller's been in the meat business since 1910. They boast that they have "The Best Tasting Hot Dogs in the World." If you don't believe them, ask the Oakland Raider fans who devour them by the thousands at the Oakland football arena.

This recipe comes from Miller's web page, and is a unique recipe for hot dogs. It just shows what a little imagination can do to make a great wiener even greater!

8 Miller's Brand Colossal Beef Franks. (If you can't get Miller's, substitute another quality beef wiener). Cut three 1/4 inch deep slits on each side of hot dogs. Place in a 2-1/2 quart baking dish. Pour Miller's Hot Dog Barbecue Sauce (see page 34) over the wieners. Cover and bake at 350 degrees for 40 – 45 minutes. Remove from oven, place in buns. Spoon extra sauce over dogs.

NEW YORK STREET VENDOR DOG

It's risky business to say that any one hot dog is typical of New York City. There are just too many variables, ethnic groups and regional tastes in this great City to attempt a rigid definition of what is typical. Odds are that somewhere in New York City, a person could find a clone of just about every hot dog recipe published in this book. So, if I offend your culinary sensibilities by calling this version of a hot dog a "New York Street Vendor Dog" . . . I apologize.

Now, with that said, here's a recipe for making a hot dog that's topped with either a boiled or a pan fried onion sauce.

Steam bun. Boil wiener of your choice. Place in the bun; add a stream of ballpark-type mustard. Top with either the Hot Dog Onion Sauce found on page 38 or the NYC Push Cart Hotdog Relish on page 37.

PIZZA DOG

We're talking about adding a little Italian flavor to what is basically a German recipe. O.K., now, don't turn up your nose. In the fancy cookbooks, it's called fusion cooking. I prefer to call it "confusion" since Mediterranean cooking and European cooking are pretty far apart. But don't judge a dog by its cover! It's what's inside that counts.

You'll notice we've also taken a couple of liberties with the "wiener" in this recipe. It's not a traditional dog, but an Italian sausage that's sized like a frankfurter. Oh, well, that's enough persuading. Enjoy!

Use an Italian sausage or other spicy sausage that is approximately the size of a traditional wiener. Remember, you're putting it inside a hot dog bun. Grill or pan fry the sausage. Place in bun, spoon on the Pizza Dog Sauce from page 40. Sprinkle on a layer of shredded mozzarella cheese and some hot pepper rings. Now, that's Italian!

TOLEDO DOG

Toledo is home to Tony Packo's, an eatery made famous by Klinger on the popular CBS TV show M*A*S*H. Folks who call this Ohio city home knew all along that the hot dogs at Tony Packo's were something special.

So popular was the hot dog served up by this Toledo restaurant that several people have tried to duplicate their sauce . . . none very successfully, I might add. None-the-less, here's a great hot dog patterned *loosely* after the dog that Klinger made famous.

Use a spicy wiener or sausage (I buy Polish sausage the size of wieners) instead of the traditional frankfurter. Grill it or otherwise cook it your favorite way. Place it in a steamed bun. Spread a little mustard on top. Add the Toledo Hot Dog Sauce found on page 25. Top with chopped onions. Welcome to Toledo.

VEGAN DOG

This one's for all my friends who turn their noses up when I devour two loaded all-meat hot dogs at one sitting! Yes, vegetarians can enjoy an "almost" hot dog by substituting a soy wiener for the real thing, and then topping it with one of the all veggie toppings found in this book.

I'll have to admit that I'm not a fan of soy wieners, but I do have those friends who are. And, when it comes to good taste, I would never say, "It's my way or the highway!"

So, here it is . . . a tree hugger's delight!

One soy dog, grilled according to package instructions. Place in bun. Add catsup and mustard and top with either the Sauerkraut Hot Dog topping on page 43 or the Vegetarian Hot Dog sauce on page 48.

YE OLDE KRAUT DOG

Sauerkraut and wieners were a childhood favorite of mine. We'd fry the kraut in bacon grease, cut up the wieners, blend with the kraut and cook until we couldn't stand it any more. Then we would chow down!

Today's standard, the Kraut Dog, is a tasty variation of that old time delicacy. It's got a few more ingredients, but the tang of the kraut complements the spiciness of the wiener . . . . It also begs for a cold bottle of brew to be near at hand. Now, that's eating!

Boil an all beef or a pork and beef dog until done. Place in bun. Top wiener with a good dollop of yellow mustard. Then spread the Sauerkraut Hot Dog Topping printed on page 43 from edge to edge. Take a bite, then take a sip of the amber liquid. Repeat the process until hot dog is gone. Finish any remaining liquid.

SIDE DISHES AND DESSERTS TO ROUND OUT THE MEAL

ON THE SIDE

If you gotta have something on the side of your hot dog plate, here are a few suggestions. Of course you can always skip the side dish and eat another hot dog. I guess that's why they're called side dishes and not entrees!

The choices for sides are pretty easy. No reason to get fancy . . . . Choose potato salads, macaroni salads, baked or barbecued beans, potato chips or the standard of most fast food restaurants, French fried potatoes. Ditto for desserts. Simple cobblers, fruit pies, or just plain fruit—in my humble opinion—are the best choices.

ALL AMERICAN MACARONI SALAD

8 oz. uncooked elbow macaroni
1 cup salad dressing
1/2 cup finely chopped celery
1/4 cup minced onion
2 tbs. sweet pickle relish
3/4 tsp. dry ground mustard
salt & pepper to taste

Cook macaroni according to package directions. Rinse under cold water until pasta is cool. Drain excess water. Put cooked macaroni in a two quart bowl. In a separate bowl, blend the salad dressing, celery, onion, relish, mustard and salt and pepper. Mix with fork to blend. Add to macaroni, and toss well. Refrigerate for at least one hour. Makes 4 – 6 servings.

PASTA SALAD ITALIANO

8 oz. uncooked pasta shapes
2 tbs. chopped green onions
1/2 cup tomatoes, diced
1/4 cup chopped celery
1/4 cup chopped carrot
1/4 cup black olive slices
1/4 cup chopped red or green bell
    pepper
2 tbs. grated Romano cheese
salt & pepper to taste
1/3 cup plus 2 tbs. Italian salad dressing

Cook pasta according to package directions. Drain and rinse until pasta is cool. Toss pasta to remove excess water. Place pasta in a 2 quart serving bowl. Add the remaining ingredients, putting the Italian salad dressing on last. Toss well. Chill. Makes 6 servings.

HARRY'S POTATO SALAD

5 – 6 medium potatoes
1/4 cup salad dressing
2 tbs. sour cream
1 tbs. dry ranch dressing
2 tbs. red wine vinegar
2 tbs. milk
1 tsp. turmeric
1 tsp. granulated sugar
3 eggs, boiled hard
1/4 tsp. ground celery seed
1/4 cup chopped onions
2 tbs. minced sweet pickles
salt & pepper to taste
4 strips bacon, fried and crumbled
pinch of paprika
sprig of parsley for garnish

Peel and boil potatoes (You can leave the skins on while boiling, then remove if you prefer). Cool and cut into 1/2" cubes. Chop two of the boiled eggs. Add to potatoes. Add celery seed, onion and pickle. Stir gently to blend. Combine salad dressing, sour cream, dry ranch dressing, wine vinegar, milk, turmeric and sugar in a separate bowl. Blend well. Add dressing to the potato mixture. Add salt and pepper to taste. Toss gently with rubber spatula. Top with crumbled bacon and one boiled egg, which has been sliced. Garnish with paprika and parsley. Makes 6 – 8 servings.

EASY POTATO SALAD

1 can (15 oz.) cooked, diced potatoes
2 eggs, hard boiled
2 tbs. chopped onion
2 tbs. sweet pickle relish
1 six-inch stalk celery, finely chopped
1/4 cup mayonnaise
1 tbs. yellow mustard
1 tbs. granulated sugar
2 tbs. milk

Drain potatoes. Place in 2 quart serving bowl. Chop the boiled eggs, add to potatoes. Gently blend in the chopped onion, relish, and chopped celery. In a smaller bowl, blend the mayonnaise, mustard, sugar and milk. Whip with a fork until well mixed. Add enough dressing to potato mixture to coat the potatoes. Toss gently with a rubber spatula. You may want to reserve some of the dressing for another occasion. Makes 4 servings.

COLE SLAW DRESSING

(Courtesy of Grandma Prelaz,
Founder of Prelaz Restaurant in Richwood, WV)

1/3 cup sugar
1/3 cup distilled vinegar
1 tsp. salt
1 tsp. pepper
1 tsp. celery seed
1 cup vegetable oil
1 quart Miracle Whip

Mix together the first five ingredients. Important that they are mixed well. Add the oil and mix well. Add the Miracle Whip and again mix very well. Use for cabbage slaw or macaroni salad.

EASY BAKED BEANS

4 slices bacon, fried crisp
1/2 cup chopped onion
2 one pound cans pork and beans in
    tomato sauce
2 tbs. brown sugar
1 tbs. Worcestershire sauce
1 tsp. prepared mustard

Sautée onions in bacon grease. Put beans in a 2 quart ovenproof casserole. Add the onions, bacon grease, brown sugar, Worcestershire sauce, mustard and bacon (crumbled). Mix well. Cover. Place in a 350 degree oven for approximately one hour. Remove cover the last 30 minutes of the bake. Makes 6 – 8 servings.

BUNK HOUSE BEANS

2 (15 oz.) cans cooked pinto beans
1/2 cup diced tomatoes
1/2 medium onion, chopped
2 slices bacon, chopped
2 tbs. brown sugar
1 tbs. chili powder
1 tbs. Worcestershire sauce
1 tsp. cumin powder
1/2 tsp. garlic powder
1 small can, chopped green chilies
1/2 lb. smoked, cooked sausage link
salt & pepper to taste

Place beans in a two quart saucepan. Add the remaining ingredients, except the sausage. Bring to a slight boil, reduce heat and simmer for 20-25 minutes. Slice sausage link into 1/4 inch pieces. Add to beans. Cook for another 10 minutes. Makes 6 – 8 servings.

APPLE CRISP

4 cups sliced tart apples
3/4 cup brown sugar
1/2 cup all purpose flour
1/2 cup old fashioned oats
3/4 tsp. cinnamon
3/4 tsp. nutmeg
1/3 cup butter or margarine, softened

Preheat oven to 350 degrees. Grease an 8 x 8 x 2" square pan. Place apple slices in pan. Mix remaining ingredients thoroughly. Sprinkle over apples. Bake 30 minutes or until apples are tender and top is golden brown. Serve warm with cream or ice cream. Makes 6 servings.

STRAWBERRY SHORTCAKE

4 cups sliced strawberries
1/2 cup sugar
2 1/3 cups Bisquick
1/2 cup milk
3 tbs. sugar
3 tbs. butter or margarine, melted
store-bought whipped cream

Mix strawberries and sugar. Set aside. Preheat oven to 450 degrees. Stir Bisquick, milk, sugar and butter together until soft dough forms. Drop by six spoonfuls onto an ungreased cookie sheet. Bake 10 – 12 minutes or until tops are golden brown. Split warm shortcakes, top with strawberries and whipped cream. Makes 6 servings.

SO, YOU WANT TO MAKE YOUR OWN WIENERS!

CALL THEM FRANKFURTERS, WIENERS OR LITTLE DACHSHUND SAUSAGES, YOU CAN MAKE YOUR OWN, IF YOU DARE!

A few years back I ordered frankfurter seasoning from a company in Texas. I was going to make my own wieners, and, hopefully, impress my friends and family. A few weeks ago, I threw that seasoning away. It had gone bad, gotten as hard as a rock. My good intentions were like that road that leads to Hades, or worse.

Sometime before that, I received a copy of a recipe for making your own frankfurters, complete with nutritional data. I punched it and placed it in my three hole notebook for future reference. It has now turned yellow from non-use.

My point is that I consider myself a connoisseur when it comes to hot dogs, but I'm not so much a purist that I have to make my own. There are a lot of great tasting wieners on the grocery shelves. I'll opt for them until someone convinces me that making your own frankfurters is both time saving and economical, as well as superior in taste. Even at my age, we had store bought wieners when I was a kid. I plan to be true to my childhood memories. But, there are those among us who'd rather do it themselves. I salute you, and herewith offer you a recipe for homemade frankfurters.

HOMEMADE WIENERS

1 lb. lean, boneless beef, cut into cubes
1 lb. lean, boneless pork, cut into cubes
1/2 lb. pork fat (chilled)
2 tbs. onion powder
1/2 tsp. garlic powder
1/4 tsp. ground mace
1/4 tsp. ground marjoram
1/2 tsp. ground mustard
1 tsp. finely ground pepper
1 tsp. granulated sugar
1 tsp. salt
1 egg white, slightly beaten
1/4 cup whole milk
12 casings, prepared according to label

Finely grind the beef. Then do the same with the pork. Finally, finely grind the pork fat, which has been chilled. Combine all three, then grind a second time or process in a food processor until well blended and mixture is near paste-like. Add the seasonings, egg white and milk to the mixture, and process again. Place in refrigerator and let chill for one hour. Stuff loosely in the prepared casings, tying off each link at 6 inches. Check to see if any air has been trapped in the stuffed casings. If so, prick with a pin or skewer to remove. Simmer the frankfurters in boiling water for 30 minutes. Remove and place in ice water to chill quickly. Drain, and refrigerate for up to 7 days. May be frozen. Prepare your favorite way. Makes 10 – 12 wieners.

HEY, HOT DOG GUY! FREQUENTLY ASKED QUESTIONS.

QUESTIONS FREQUENTLY ASKED OF THE HOT DOG GUY

Dear Mr. Hot Dog,
What is the best wiener to use when making hot dogs?

—B.B.

Dear B.B.,

The best wiener is the one you like best. Of course you have choices of all beef, all pork, beef and pork, chicken and pork, turkey and pork, all chicken and the soy dog. Although I haven't seen one, there's probably a wiener on the market that contains beef, pork, chicken and soy filler!

I do have my favorites, but I don't believe in forcing my culinary opinions on strangers. To be completely honest, the all beef wiener seems to get the nod from so-called gourmets. A quick look in the grocery store aisle, however, would indicate that the home consumer prefers the combination of chicken and pork. At least, there are more brands with those ingredients listed taking up space in the cooler. It's not your grandfather's frankfurter, but folks seem to like them. I suggest you try different brands and meat combinations, and choose your favorite . . . not a bad assignment considering that there are dozens and dozens of options.

Hey, Hot Dog Guy,

Explain the differences in the buns used for hot dogs.

— E.K.

Dear E.K.,

There are basically three different styles of buns on the market. Some are combinations of different flours, such as whole wheat or potato flour mixed with processed flour. However, it is the shape and style of the bun that gets our attention.

We are all familiar with the 8 and 12 packs of hot dog buns most bread companies produce. Usually they sell for 12-15 cents apiece, are split down the center and are barely large enough to hold a wiener with all of its toppings. They are none-the-less a good value and a popular choice.

The next most common hot dog bun is what is called either the English or New England style bun. It looks more like a rectangle, generally is split down the center and is frequently packaged in smaller quantities. The advantage to the English bun is that the sides are left touching when baking and are not browned. Consequently, it lends itself to toasting on both sides, a nice treat, especially if you are grilling outside. By the way, English style buns are slightly more expensive than the traditional buns discussed above.

The third style is the freshly baked deli style hot dog bun. It is usually fresher, may or may not be split, and will not be as uniform in size. If bread is your thing, however, you'll opt for the just-baked bun to complement your hot dog. When it comes to bread, fresh always tastes best.

There are other variations, such as poppy seed or sesame seed buns. Indeed, the Chicago Style Hot Dog recipe published in this book calls specifically for a poppy seed bun. They're hard to find outside of metropolitan areas, but if you're lucky enough to find some, buy 'em and enjoy them.

Yo, Hot Dog Dude,
Like man, which sauce is best to use when my "bros" are coming to visit?
— B.D.

Dear B.D.,

You've got more choices in toppings than you have in types of wieners. It all depends on where you live and what you remember growing up as a kid—I assume you have grown up.

Meat sauces, such as the Coney Island type are popular in the Northeast, the South and out West. In the Heartland, veggie toppings with pickle relish, hot peppers and mustard are favorites. If you are a risk taker, try one of the more exotic recipes, i.e., Hawaiian Hot Dog Sauce or the Miller's Barbecue Sauce.

Don't be lulled into thinking that all meat sauce recipes are alike. Some are sweet, some spicy; others have a strong tomato base, while a few have little or no tomatoes in them. You can crank up the heat on any of the meat recipes by adding crushed red pepper, cayenne pepper or a Louisiana hot sauce.

Then there are the grilled onion types of toppings, which are popular in parts of the North. Blended with mustard and other seasonings, these sauces can be a pleasant surprise to the palate.

Best bet? If you have friends (or "bros") coming to dinner, give them a choice of two or three. Let them decide which topping they like best.

Dear Wizard of the Weenie,
Can I substitute ground pork, chicken, turkey or lamb for the beef in the meat sauce? What about soy lookalikes?

— P.K.

Dear P.K.,
Short answer is "yes." But, and it's a significant but, you'll have to adjust cooking times. Ground chicken and turkey tend to break up with long cooking times. Pork on the other hand holds up pretty well. Ditto for lamb. Soy "lookalikes" require an entirely different approach. Most manufacturers suggest adding the soy crumbles at the end of the cooking. Obviously, the recipes in which substitutions are made will not taste quite the same as the original, but to each his own.

Dear Frank,
Which chili powder should I use?

—J.J.

Dear J.J.,
The easy answer is to use the chili powder you normally use. However, there is some risk in doing

that since chili powders vary greatly in taste.

Chances are the chili powder used in most of the meat sauce recipes in this book are variations of what is called "processor's choice" in the trade. The most recognizable brand of this type of powder is McCormick's, which has been a staple for a long time. There are other choices that would work as well, and these would be mostly "store" brands and mixes from other lesser known producers who blend and distribute chili powders which are similar to McCormick's. Be leery of off-brand chili powders that list salt as their first ingredient. Always look for the words "chili peppers."

Dear Dog Doctor,

Is it ok to brown the meat before adding the liquid ingredients?

— H.G.

Dear H.G.,

Many people do indeed brown their meat before adding the liquid ingredients. But, in my opinion, you sacrifice taste and texture when you do. One thing I learned early while doing research for this book was that restaurants, which are known for their hot dogs, always boil their ground beef before adding the other seasonings. Sometimes, they would add minced onions, but the chili powder, pepper and tomato sauces or pastes were added later.

Another point I need to make is that ground beef— we call it hamburger—is used almost exclusively.

I never saw a restaurant recipe for hot dog chili that was made with ground chuck or round. Frankly, it doesn't contain enough fat to give the hot dog sauce the flavor and consistency it needs to spread evenly over the wiener. Most hot dogs have less than one ounce of chili sauce on them. There's little reason to quibble over the scant amount of fat you're going to get in the sauce. You're better off to celebrate the flavor the fat adds!

Hey Hot Dog Guy,

How big is a serving? You keep mentioning that a sauce recipe makes 20 or 30 servings . . . .I need some help.

—J.H.

Dear J.H.,

Great question! I'm afraid my answer won't be as good. Serving sizes are estimates. It all depends on how much sauce or topping you personally like on your hot dog.

A pound of ground beef, mixed with a couple cups of water and a 15 ounce can of tomato sauce, cooked slowly for 2 hours, will yield enough sauce for 20+ hot dogs. Cook the sauce longer, and the yield goes down. Add more liquid, and the yield increases. In other words, it's a guess . . . and, as they say back home, your guess is as good as mine!

Best advice is to make extra, and freeze it. It will keep up to 3 months in the freezer.

INDEX

SAUCES:

RESTAURANT HOT DOGS:

LET'S MAKE HOT DOGS:

SIDE DISHES: